D1579601

*pocket guides*

# CHINA TEAPOTS

*Pottery and Porcelain*

by

Pauline Agius

*Series Editor:* Noël Riley

LUTTERWORTH PRESS
Guildford, Surrey

*First published 1982*

Cover illustration shows
a Coalport teapot
(John Rose) *c.* 1803—7.

*For Carolyn, Andrew and Alicia*

ISBN 0 7188—2548—9

Printed in Great Britain by
Mackays of Chatham Ltd

# Contents

1. (*above*) Late 17th century Yi Hsing stoneware.   (*below*) Wedgwood shape 146 still in production after two centuries.

# Introduction

OVER the last three centuries teapots have provided potters and designers with so many challenging choices of outline, moulding, handle, lid, spout and decoration that they now provide a rich, complex and sculpturally exciting collecting subject. Teapots challenge the potter to create a pleasing object out of a body with two holes, a lid and a handle. These elements, which must perform the practical functions of withstanding and holding boiling water and enabling the tea to be poured in a steady stream, challenge the potter to creative solutions. A good deal of our enjoyment of a fine pot surely comes from the successful fusion of function and form in teapots, like those in fig. 1, which simply ask to be picked up and poured from.

But a good deal of the entertainment in teapot collecting can come, rather differently, from discovering how closely teapots are related to the decorative themes, motifs and fashions of their time. Think, for example, of the cube teapots of the 1930s, at one with the

2. An oval backed chair of the late 18th century.

3. An oval shaped tomb, late 18th century.

5

4. (*right* and *far right*)
Further examples of the late
18th century.

cubist light fittings and square chunky arm-
chairs of the period. Similarly the many oval
teapots at the end of the 18th century followed
the fashionable oval backed chairs, much
silver and even tombs as in figs. 2, 3 and 4(a)
and (b). James Laver wrote of this quirky
'time spirit':

'. . . it does seem as if there were, at any
given time, a mould into which the imagin-
ation of the age is compelled to pour itself,
with the result that everything that is produced in that age is, more or less of the same
shape, even when any question of conscious
style is ruled out. It is as if a mad cook
should restrict himself to one tin or patty
pan whether he was making a blancmange
or a game pie. Some of the substances he
pours into it keep the shape of the mould
better than others, some things jell more
easily than others, but in all of them we can
recognize the family likeness'.

In addition to the aesthetic appeal and the
entertainment value of teapot collecting there

are, of course, the pleasures of the chase and the great satisfaction to be had from the detective work entailed in discovering when, where and by whom an unmarked teapot was made.

Perhaps you are not a teapot collector but rather, simply want to enjoy a few shapes on a shelf or to include the occasional teapot in a collection based on a wider theme. But if you are intending to be a teapot specialist, you will probably be aiming at a collection which shows as much as possible of the whole range of development of teapot design. As this little book aims to be practical and realistic, we must face the situation that now, in the late 20th century, historic ceramics are expensive and scarce. Fig. 5 shows one of the most expensive teapots, a rare Venetian Vezzi, sold at Christie's for £17,000; fig. 6 shows a type of Worcester soft paste which could cost anything between £200 and £2,000 depending on decoration and condition.

If you have considerable finances, a more than average ration of luck and a fairly long-

5. Rare Venetian Vezzi about 1725, £17,000 at Christie's.

6. Soft paste blue scale ground Worcester c. 1770. Price £200–£2,000, depending on condition and decoration.

term affair with teapots, you will still be able to make a desirable evolutionary collection. But if cash is somewhat lacking, you will have to accept some chipped spouts, lidless pots, damaged knobs and mended handles. Such flaws are acceptable to keen collectors who can be entranced by the delectable feel of, say, creamware, or the delicious, runny lead glaze colours or a transfer print that transports them to another age – better to have a damaged piece in your hands than to be kept at a distance by a museum case. But, except where the damaged pieces are very rare like the one described as 'a large chip with a rare Lowestoft beaker attached' which recently fetched £320 at Christie's, they are not sound investments.

Spend only what you can easily afford to part with on these desirable but imperfect pieces. Whether you have the cash or not you will find that many of the representative examples you would like are distinctly scarce so you will have to be patient as well as active. Yet

7. Longpark, Torquay, slip decorated, 1905–13.

collecting should provide fun and satisfaction rather than disappointment and woe; and the way to bypass the frustration is to form at the same time a second specialist collection in a narrower field which has not yet been over searched. Items in figs. 7 and 8 were each bought for £5 or less in 1981. Although there is a vast amount of knowledge and a rich array of deeply researched ceramic literature, yet there is a great deal we do not know about who made what, where and when. There are challenges at all levels, whether you want to burrow in old trade directories and pattern books, or join a dig on an old factory site, or compare the work of different decorators, or, simply, seek and search wherever antique shop, junk shop, auction or jumble sale can be found.

You will find an informative survey and some coloured illustrations in Henry Sandon's *Coffee Pots and Teapots for the Collector*. Absolutely essential, for its hundreds of outline diagrams illustrating the differences

8. Wedgwood bone china 1930.

between similar pots made by different factories, is Philip Miller's *Teapots and Coffee Pots*. Less detailed but delectably readable is John Bedford's out of print *Talking about Teapots* which radiates the enthusiasm of the hooked collector. More expensive but invaluable, and you will certainly find yourself buying it sooner or later, so the sooner the better, is Geoffrey Godden's *Illustrated Encyclopaedia of British Pottery and Porcelain*. You will certainly frequently need to consult his companion volume: *The Encyclopaedia of British Pottery and Porcelain Marks*.

Chapter 1 will provide an outline history of teapots to the present but this little book must commend to you the existing literature (*see* pp. 61–62) for the more detailed information you need, so that it can concentrate more usefully, in Chapter 2, on what kind of specialist collections can still be made and in Chapter 3 on the practicalities of collecting: what to notice, where to look and learn and how to identify.

# 1. An Outline History of Teapots

WHEN tea was first imported into England from the middle of the 17th century, little terracotta red, hard stoneware teapots came with it. They varied from the spherical and elegantly simple (fig. 1) to elaborately encrusted shapes like fig. 9 or sections of a branch with twig attachments.

We do not know who made the first English pots but before the end of the 17th century fine quality unglazed red stonewares were being made in London and by the Elers brothers in Staffordshire. Very few teapots seem to remain from before the 1740s. It is difficult both to date these pots and to distinguish between the imports, made over a long period, and our copies. A representative collection should

9. Hexagonal red stoneware.

10. Red stoneware c.1750 with applied 'sprigging', crabstock handle and spout.

11. Tin-glazed delftware
*c*.1740, painted in blue.

12. Painted salt-glaze
*c*.1750–60.

include one, but you will almost certainly have to be content with it being of uncertain date and attribution.

**The Golden Age of English Earthenware.**

13. Brown lead-glaze, mid-18th century.

By the 1740s many potters, like the renowned Astburys, had experimented with many clays and different glazes and what is now considered the golden age was dawning. As well as the unglazed red stonewares like fig. 10, there were the easily damaged, white, tin-glazed delft wares (fig. 11), the fine salt-glazed stonewares (fig. 12) and the lead-glazed earthenwares (fig. 17).

The story of teapots is very much the tale of the different body materials which potters have developed and of the opportunities these have offered.

14. Salt-glazed stoneware 'house' *c*.1740.

**Salt-glazed Stonewares.** The finely ground flint and pale clays for rounded salt-glazed pots could be thrown and shaped on the potter's wheel but for complex shapes, like the house in fig. 14, the clay was thinned to a liquid 'slip' and poured into plaster of Paris moulds which had themselves been formed from hard and elaborately carved master moulds. It is worth looking briefly at the process because it continued to be a standard method. After a time some of the water from the 'slip' is absorbed by the plaster and leaves a thin layer of clay against the mould. The remaining liquid is then poured out and when the thin layer of clay has hardened sufficiently, the mould – in two or three pieces – is removed and the pot is left to harden further. During the firing in the kiln, salt is left to vaporize. It reacts with the silica present in the body of the stoneware to form a thin glaze on the surface of the pot. Moulded teapots like fig. 14 need no further decoration but some like the pecten shell pear shape (fig. 15) were painted, as were thrown pots (fig. 16).

**Lead-glazed Earthenware.** Before the 1740s there were brown and the black, known as

15. Salt-glazed four-lobed moulded pear shape *c*.1750.

16. (*left*) Globular salt-glazed body painted in black *c*.1755.   17. (*right*) Lead-glazed earthenware 'pineapple' *c*.1760.

'Jackfield' lead-glazed earthenwares, but colour was a great challenge to many potters. In the 1750s Thomas Whieldon and the first Josiah Wedgwood perfected some richly coloured lead glazes to decorate their increasingly well potted earthenwares. Some of their jolly teapots, sometimes in the shape of fruit or vegetables (fig. 17), look as if they are coated with runny greengage jam and golden syrup. Others like fig. 18 were decorated with 'sprigging'. Some of the colourful pots, as in fig. 19, were made from the elaborate salt-glaze

18. Globular lead-glazed brown body with applied 'sprigging' *c*.1760.

19. (*left*) Lead-glazed hexagon, leaf handle and spout, Chinese figures in panels, mainly green and yellow *c.*1760.    20. (*right*) Lead-glazed solid agate ware with lion knob and paw feet *c.*1750.

moulds. The whole range, made by many potters, is often referred to as 'Whieldon/ Wedgwood'. Fig. 20 shows an alternative body, one of the attractive agate ware pots made by mixing several coloured clays, which thus create their own pattern.

But having looked at the beginnings of this 'golden age of English earthenware' up to the 1760s we have rushed ahead too fast and skipped over one of the most important chapters in ceramic history: early European porcelains.

21. Important, rare Böttger polished red stoneware. Meissen 1710–15, £30,000 at Phillips.

## Porcelains

(a) *True hard paste.* The impressive oriental porcelains which, in addition to tea and stoneware teapots, had reached the courts of Europe in quantity by the end of the 17th century century, intoxicated their owners and viewers. People were entranced by the fine forms and decoration, its hardness and especially its whiteness, translucency and glassy finish. But it was very expensive so urgent searches and experiments started with the aim of home production. The story of how Augustus the Strong of Saxony first imprisoned a brilliant chemist, Böttger, to force him to concentrate on turning base metals into gold so that Augustus would be able to afford the porcelain, and then directed him rather to seek how to make the porcelain itself, should

22. Meissen true porcelain, gilded and painted with Chinese scenes, 1720s.

23. Worcester moulded fluted body with scroll edge panels, Fisherman and Willow Pavilion pattern, *c.* 1755–60.

24. (*left*) Hexagonal Worcester with loop handle and flower knop 1770s. (*right*) Worcester painted with Chinese figures, 1760s.

be read in full. Böttger first produced fine red stoneware (fig. 21) and then *c.* 1710 actually managed to make true hard paste porcelain in the oriental manner, by firing china clay and china stone at high temperatures. Thus the great Meissen factory came into being and almost from the start produced such fine shapes and decoration that it seems as if European hard paste porcelain was born fully matured (fig. 22).

(b) *Soft paste porcelain.* But the secret of how to make this true hard paste porcelain eluded most of the searchers. In England, France and elsewhere a substitute known as 'soft paste' porcelain was evolved. It was fairly white and translucent but not so durable and not so highly fired. You can see the difference if you look at chipped items under a magnifying glass. The hard paste will have conchoidal fractures like hard toffee whereas the soft paste will look gritty like a fine biscuit. Hard paste feels cold and glassy if you hold it against your cheek, while soft paste feels more like new toilet soap, and soon becomes warmer. Even so, it is not always easy to distinguish undamaged items.

25. Worcester blue scale ground with painted panels, mid-1760s onwards.

26. Two Worcesters transfer printed in black, 1760s.

This substitute soft paste, proved to have distinct advantages and led to half a century of delightful, lovable English, French and other porcelains like figs. 23 and 24(a) and (b). As they did not need to be so highly fired the cobalt blues applied under the glaze remained in rich tones and the smooth lead glaze married happily with the soft paste to provide a glowing luminosity which is quite different from that of the glossy hard paste. Like Meissen the early French and English factories seem to have been so pleased with the actual

27. Worcester fluted barrel-shape painted and gilded mid-1770s.

body paste they produced that, although they did copy some complex oriental shapes like the Chelsea cabbage teapot, they preferred in the main to concentrate on rounded teapots which showed off the body porcelain to good advantage.

The English soft paste factories, whose teapots you will see, were Bow, Chelsea, Worcester, Derby, Caughley, Liverpool, Longton Hall and Newcastle-under-Lyme. Figs. 25 to 27 provide more examples. Some are marked, but attributions usually depend on combinations of characteristics, such as the shape of the handle, whether Worcester's plain or ribbed loop or Derby's pixie ear; by the shade of the translucency: duck egg or straw; by the

28. Plymouth hard paste *c.*1768.

29. Creamware, Melbourne type, 1760s–70s, double intertwined handle, diaper pattern in iron red and black.

30. Creamware inverted pear shape with pierced gallery, probably Staffordshire *c.*1775.

19

31. Creamware, Leeds
pottery late 1770s–80s with
portrait of John Wesley.

32. (*above*) Wedgwood
white jasper sage green dip,
cylindrical 'Brewster'
shape, 1780s.
(*below*) Wedgwood blue
and white jasper with
'Spinner' relief *c*.1790.

knob of the lid, whether a well-moulded Worcester flower sitting close to the lid, or the later Worcester stud-like knob. The whole subject is enjoyably and teasingly complex but has become expensive. It can best be followed up in Bernard Watney's *English Blue and White Porcelain of the 18th century* which provides a great deal of information about the factories as well as their blue and white products.

Experiments to make the true hard paste porcelain continued and in 1768 a Quaker apothecary, William Cookworthy, working in Plymouth, actually succeeded. He later continued production in Bristol. Fig. 28 shows a typical example but, of course, not many are available. His patent, in theory, prevented other porcelain makers from using the petuntse or china stone which was the key ingredient but undoubtedly some did experiment with it. From 1781 a considerable quantity of hard paste (fig. 38) continued to be made in Staffordshire by the New Hall Company, which had bought the patent rights.

**Creamware.** Spurred on by the successes of the porcelain makers, the potters had been refining their wares and a good many by the

1760s and 70s were producing desirably fine lightweight cream-coloured earthenwares no longer hidden under thick lead glazes. It was Josiah Wedgwood who popularized the names creamware and Queensware, when in 1765 a tea service of this type of fine earthenware was supplied to and named after Queen Charlotte. The firm of Wedgwood, the Leeds and other Yorkshire Potteries and some in Derbyshire and Staffordshire produced large quantities, much of which was exported. A selection of creamware teapot shapes are shown in figs. 29 to 31. This body is surprisingly light: for example, a two pint creamware teapot can weigh less than fourteen ounces. There are many different knobs of lids and handle terminals but there was a great deal of copying between factories, so there is still plenty of confusion. The so-called 'Melbourne type' teapot (fig. 29), for example, still awaits conclusive attribution. Some makers of cream-

33. Wedgwood caneware c.1796.

34. Blackware: Leeds or Turner, Staffs., 1800–20, swan knop on sliding lid.

35. Blackware variant on London shape 1810–20s with vines, strawberries and gadrooning.

36. White felspathic stoneware, outlined in blue, yellow and green c.1800–20.

ware in the last quarter of the 18th century and later produced a fine white version of creamware known as *pearlware*, presumably to compete with the blue and white porcelains. This is less collected than creamware and should be less expensive but not too much seems to be available. Perhaps demand by collectors would smoke it out.

**Dry Bodies.** These appeared during the same period and like the early red stoneware, did not need to be glazed. They were notable competitors to creamware teapots and much more robust. *Jasperware*, a very fine, hard body which was regarded as one of Wedgwood's triumphs, is shown in figs. 32(a) and (b). A similar body, buff-tinted and moulded is known as *caneware* (fig. 33). *Blackware*, or, as Wedgwood called it, *Basalte*, was made from the 1760s but the most interesting teapots in this astonishingly hard body seem to have

a

b

c

d

e

f

37. Here is a page of illustrations to reassure you that you can recognize various types of 18th century teapots. Quiz provided by Phillips Auctioneers.
*Solutions on p. 63*

38. Fluted New Hall
'commode' silver shape,
pattern 202, c.1787–95.

39. Straight sided Old
Oval with faceted spout,
Coalport c.1805.

40. Minton New Oval
'canoe' monochrome hand-
painted c.1810.

been made from the 1790s–1820s, as shown in figs. 34 and 35. Its colour was thought to flatter the hands of the pourer. Notice the sharpness of the elaborate moulding, undiminished by a glaze. Blackware has never been as popular as creamware but can be very fine and cherishable. *White Felspathic Stoneware* teapots are often referred to as 'Castleford', but they were made in several places. They were sometimes made from the same moulds as blackware. Fig. 36 has a scene from classical mythology on one side and a tavern scene on the other.

It was in *porcelains*, however, that the most notable developments took place at the end of the 18th century. The brave experimental soft paste factories, some flourishing, some bankrupt, had produced an impressive range of desirable wares in blue and white and with polychrome decoration before this type of porcelain was mainly superseded in the 1790s. By then J. Spode I and others had evolved very white and translucent *bone china* which was more reliably reproducible. It contained ground animal bones as well as the china clay and china stone. It is fortunate for teapot collectors that from this time, when the body paste became more standard and therefore less significant, the shapes of the teapots became more varied and interesting. Of

41. New Oval tea-set, T. Rose, Coalport *c.*1810–14.

course the 'time spirit' was also at work, but presumably when makers had fewer worries about the composition of the body paste, they had time to think more about the shape the teapot should have.

**The Oval.** During the 1790s teapots began to follow the taste which had existed for over a decade in fashionable chair backs and silver, and assumed the oval shape. This was a promising direction as so many variations are possible. Fig. 4(a) has 'shankered' shoulders and ribbed fluting. A few firms, notably New

42. Minton London shape painted and gilded, pattern 678 *c.*1810–25.

43. (*left*) Wedgwood smear-glazed drabware in 1817 catalogue.
44. (*right*) Glazed Egyptian blackware 1820s and 30s.

Hall with its hard paste skills, made teapots (fig. 28), inspired by the 'commode' shape fashionable in contemporary silver and so-called because of its undulating outline in plan.

It was an exciting time of increased production. As Pitt had lowered the duty on tea in 1784 and increased that on silver plate there was greater demand for pottery and porcelain teapots in which to brew the cheaper

45. (*left*) A continental veilleuse.

46. (*right*) A taller round pot in Swansea porcelain.

drink. The Napoleonic Wars cut the import of continental porcelain and the East India Company ceased to import oriental porcelains in any quantity. So the growing Minton, Spode, Coalport, Miles Mason and New Hall factories as well as the older Wedgwood, Worcester and other firms expanded production and vied with each other to attract buyers. Fig. 39 shows the straight sides of Old Oval, popular *c.* 1795–1805; fig. 40 the curvaceous 'canoe' or New Oval, *c.* 1805–15; fig. 41 another variation of the New Oval and fig. 42 the usually squatter 'London' shape, a curved oblong in plan *c.* 1810–25. The ovals combine to form one of the most challenging groups of pots as so many factories were making them with only slight variations and few marks.

But nothing remains high fashion for too long, and although the London shapes were popular until the later 1820s, by 1815 round shapes were returning to favour. Some factories had continued to make the old rounds throughout the oval period but many of the rounds that came to be high fashion in the 1820s were squatter, like contemporary silverware (figs. 43 and 44). A taller high fashion

47. A new shape with scalloped edge made by Ridgway, Rockingham, Coalport and others, *c.* 1830.

48. Rockingham with leaf moulding and mouth spout, with matching plate and jug, late 1820s and 30s.

49. (*top*) Rockingham set, with feet and crown knop, 1830s. (*below left*) Skirted rococo sprigged and gilded on its stand, 1830s. (*below right*) Grainger's rococo, *c*.1839.

example in Swansea porcelain is shown in fig. 46.

The veilleuse or drink warmer, shown in fig. 45, has been a popular continental product since the mid-18th century but less so here. Minton and Wedgwood made attractive examples with squat pots around 1820.

**Neo-Rococo.** A dignified new shape made by Rockingham and Ridgway, among others, is shown in fig. 47. This is more sober than most of the rococo revival shapes of the 1830s and 40s. The 1820s had fostered a more lively, robust taste in furniture with much 'vegetal vigour' in the carving and a revival of curvaceous rococo forms. This soon reached ceramics and the ubiquitous C scrolls and twists and turns so characteristic of early Victorian furniture are seen in teapots of the 1830s and 40s, as in figs. 49(a–c). Each part of the pot seems to demand attention. Spouts began to have more complex outlines, a few even ending in birds' mouths. Handles became prouder and knobs of lids larger, sometimes in the form of crowns (fig. 49(a)) or creatures. The pots often stand on feet or undulating skirts.

**Second half of the 19th century.** This period is remarkable for its variety. After the peak of neo-rococo in the 1830s and 40s china makers, like the furniture designers of the time, became too obsessed with the creations of the past. There was much traditional craftsmanship, as in fig. 50, and the pierced porcelain *tour de force* (fig. 51) by George Owen of Royal Worcester, but altogether too much concern with copying the styles of other times and other lands. There were many copies of old blue and white favourites and gilded Imari and other Japanese patterns, but the gothic revival which produced many moulded jugs in the mid-century, left us few teapots. What

50. Brown glazed Wedgwood with Greek key pattern c.1875.

51. Royal Worcester pierced porcelain by George Owen 1887 and 1890s.

52. Minton's majolica
glazed monkey holding
fruit, after a Japanese
model, 1873.

53. Minton majolica glazed
chinaman, 1874.

initiative and originality there was seems to
have gone into the production of new body
materials like Minton's white Parian, the *pâte
sur pâte* process, majolica, and Henri Deux
and Doulton's faience, impasto and Carrara
bodies. These bodies were not primarily for
useful wares, but Minton's made a few *pâte sur
pâte* teapots, Doulton's more in faience and
figs. 52 and 53 show creature pots in Minton's
majolica.

Most shapes and decorations can be found
in the grand variety performance of the second
half of the 19th century but its ceramic history
has not been adequately charted. Perhaps
collectors can help to unravel what, if any,
were the main streams and tributaries. Was
there, for example, an outbreak of bizarre pots
like the monkey and the chinaman or were
these rare specimens of a short-lived phase?

The Japanese phase, obsessed with Japanese prints, fretted furniture and fans, inspired
some unusual Anglo-Japanese teapots (figs.
54 and 55) in the 1870s and 80s. This Japanese
phase was part of the art-aesthetic movement
of the 1870s and 80s, that 'New Reformed
Faith in Art' which caused it to be trendy and
exciting to debate decoration, 'art' clothes and

54. Wedgwood Satsuma
shape decorated by Emile
Lessore *c.*1876.

'art' pottery. 'Mr "Phillistine" Jones had been forced to think about the shape of his jugs' – his teapots too, surely! Artists like the Barlows produced attractive incised designs on salt-glaze teapots for Doulton's. But on the whole the newly founded art potteries such as de Morgan's, Bretby, Burmantofts and Christopher Dresser's Linthorpe were not very concerned with tablewares. Fig. 7 shows an exception, a charming little pot with the fresh clear colours of Longpark, Torquay. Figs. 56 and 57 show strands of the end-of-century taste by Doulton's. Fig. 58 is a more unusual example of their 'Marqueterie' ware with panel painted by Ada Dennis, 1887.

Invented near the end of the century but not in production by Wedgwood until 1905–6 was the SYP, the 'Simple Yet Perfect' pot in fig. 59 which lies on its side while the tea is brewing and can isolate the tea leaves when upright. There were other inventions like Royle's Self Pourer of 1887.

**Twentieth Century.** English ceramics did not follow the continental trend, like Dutch Rozenburg and some Meissen, into the sinu-

55. W. A. Adderley's earthenware 'Shansu' 1882–83.

56. Royal Doulton 'Blue Children' print, hand-tinted, 1880s–1928.

57. Doulton 'Marqueterie' gilded, 5 in. high, c.1887–91.

58. Lambeth Art Ware, panel painted by Ada Dennis, 1887.

ous forms of art nouveau and only a few were decorated in that manner. Fig. 60 is a charming Doulton example of 1905 and fig. 61 shows four designs from the very rare Minton Secessionist range, but on the traditional plain oval shape. The British counterpart of art nouveau, 'the arts and crafts' cum 'progressive', was killed by a recession around 1907 before it had had time to flower at all fully. Factories dared not experiment so mainly kept on making the safe old favourites as can be seen in catalogues of the time. There was not much life either in the craft or the industry until the 1920s.

A valiant exception was found in the work of Denise Wren who had carried on experiment-

59. The S.Y.P. invented by the Earl of Dundonald, Wedgwood 1905/6.

50. Royal Doulton with sinuous art nouveau design, 1905.

61. Rare Minton's Secessionist ware *c.*1900.

ing and so was already working when Bernard Leach returned from his training in Japan and set up as a craftsman potter in St Ives in 1920. These pioneers, and Staite Murray, inspired by Sung stonewares, have influenced two generations of craftsmen potters.

Meanwhile, in the industry Alfred and Louise Powell, survivors from the Arts and Crafts movement, were in 1918 painting tea-pots in metallic lustres for Wedgwood and later trained girls there to decorate in freehand painting techniques. The Poole Pottery was founded in 1921 by designers and craftsmen. Slowly industrial design advanced. In 1924 the old established large-scale traditional tea-pot makers, Sadlers, produced the unusual Hexagon pot shown in fig. 62. The faceted tea-pot (fig. 63) was made in 1929. In the 1930s there were various cube pots like that in fig. 63 made for the Cunard Line by Sadlers, while others were more traditional. By the mid-1930s Midwinter's had produced their variously decorated cubist range.

The geometric forms that we have come to

62. Sadler's 'Hexagon' 1924.

think of as the most characteristic of Art Deco – so named after the great L'Exposition des Arts Decoratifs in Paris in 1925 – are not best expressed in ceramics but they inspired an interesting group. Clarice Cliff was designing in the manner for Newport Potteries in the 1920s and 30s (fig. 64) and also produced bizarre pots like 'corn cobs', which might have been made any time. Susie Cooper who had designed and decorated for Grays Pottery founded her own firm in 1930–31.

By 1934 the *Studio Year Book* was reporting

63. (*above*) Art deco group: continental (coffee?) pot with electric flash handle, cubist pot made for Cunard Line and 1929 faceted purple teapot.
64. (*below*) A Clarice Cliff breakfast set, orange ground, 1930s.

65. Wedgwood Queensware with Eric Ravilious' 'Travel' design 1940s–50s.

'form in pottery as opposed to pattern makes an increasing appeal to modern taste'. Both Wedgwood's new 'Annular' shape and one by John Poole Adams in 1932 were moulded as if made of parallel layers.

After World War Two there was more emphasis on new decoration than new shapes. A notable pot of that austere time was the traditional Wedgwood 'Jubilee' shape freshened by Eric Ravilious's 'Travel' design (fig. 65). Fig. 66, one of the most attractive pots still in production, is Minton's Haddon Hall designed by John Wadsworth in 1947. The trend after the 1951 Festival of Britain was for more streamlined shapes like J. and G. Meakin's 'Horizon' and 'Studio' teapots (fig. 67).

It is difficult to discover who led the straight-sided upright shapes to dominate the Sixties and Seventies. Midwinter produced David Queensbury's designs 'Contrast' and 'Focus' and Susie Cooper various examples including the upright oval shown in fig. 68. There was Royal Worcester's Palissy Pottery

66. Minton's Fife shape with John Wadsworth's 'Haddon Hall' pattern, 1947 and still in production.

67. J. and G. Meakin's Studio ware, 1950s.

68. Susie Cooper shape and pattern made in Wedgwood bone china with various patterns in 1960s and 70s; this is 'Corn Poppy'.

69. Royal Worcester's Palissy Pottery with Scottie Wilson decoration, mid-1960s.

70. Wedgwood bone china 'Orbit' 1968–72.

decorated with Scottie Wilson's crisp black shapes in 1965 (fig. 69), Hornsea's 'Heirloom' 1967, Portmeirion's 'Totem', Midwinter's 'Spanish Garden' 1966 and many others. Wedgwood's chaste 'Orbit', 1968–72, in bone china (fig. 70) seems to look back to the prize-winning pot of 1846 and Royal Worcester's elegant, slightly barrel-shaped 'Severn', designed by Neil French in 1969 looks back to Worcesters of the 1780s. There are also ruggedly attractive pots like Pearson's 'Genesis' stoneware Coniston and Snowdon, Hornsea's 'Brontë', Denby's 'Rondo' and the gaily painted Wood's 'Firenza' available now.

71. (*left*) By A. Caiger-Smith, Aldermaston, decorated in lime and bronze greens, 1981.   (*centre*) By David Leach, Bovey Tracey, ribbed stoneware with cane handle, 1970s.   (*right*) By Svend Bayer *c*.1978.

72. Rosenthal's 'Magic Flute' set, *c*.1979 onwards.

73. Hornsea's blackware
'Image', from 1977,
designed by Martin Hunt.

74. 'Tea-for-One' designed
by Martin Hunt.

Many craftsmen potters have been producing teapots during recent decades in a great variety of bodies and glazes from raku and pierced porcelain to tenmoku and lustres. Notable among them are: Richard Batterham, Terry Bell Hughes, Alan Caiger-Smith, Michael Cardew, Sally Dawson, Peter Dick, Wally Keeler, Colin Kellam, David Leach, Jim Malone, John Maltby, Ian Pirie, Mary Rich, Lucie Rie, Janice Tchalenko, Geoffrey Whiting, and Geoffrey and Joanna Young (fig. 71).

One of the most striking recent designs from the ceramic industry is Rosenthal's 'Magic Flute' (fig. 72). The new body material of Hornsea's sleek 'Image' (fig. 73) in the smoothest, silkiest black, matches up to the best of 18th-century blackwares. The design is by Martin Hunt who must also be credited with what is, surely, one of the wittiest teapots: 'Tea-for-One' (fig. 74).

# 2.    Alternative Specialist Collections

IT would be splendid if you could now make a shopping list of a score or so of representative teapots that you particularly liked from Chapter 1 and go forth confidently expecting to find them all in the next year or eighteen months at prices you could afford. But prices can be a deterrent and specimens scarce, so to ensure joyful and creative collecting you need to make a second collection which you can add to frequently without crippling your finances. This chapter aims to spotlight some areas in which there still seems a good deal to be found and found out about. Choose a theme which appeals to you both aesthetically and historically and go

75. Leeds Pottery blackware Old Oval with cannon spout and widow knop *c.*1795–1820.

76. Some ovals: (*above*)
Spode. (*below*) Minton
*c*.1810, pattern 1041.
(*bottom*) Derby with prow
rim *c*.1815–20 pattern 725,
*c*.1810–15?

into it as deeply as possible. It is those with
specialized knowledge who see the relevant
and can seize opportunities. Vow not to be a
magpie, buying whatever is offered that is
even vaguely attractive. That leads to mere
accumulations, not collections and deprives
others of items that might actually be relevant
to their themes.

**The Ovals** of *c*. 1790–1820 are probably the
earliest period from which many teapots are
still available and they are among the most
elegant (figs. 75 and 76 with three styles).
Many of the variants are most helpfully shown
diagrammatically in Philip Miller's *Teapots and
Coffee Pots* and perhaps nearly half of them can
be identified from pattern numbers on their
bases. The straight-sided oval as in fig. 75 is
such a desirably elegant shape that had it not
been followed by that specifically English con-
tribution to teapot design, the pleasing 'canoe'
shape, its passing would have been more
lamented (fig. 76 *top* and *centre*).

It would be enlightening to discover a reference in a novel or diary of the time indicating
how these shapes were received. Did the old
round shapes seem very old fashioned before
1800 but then pleasantly new again a little
before 1820? It is information like this that
needs to be pursued as well as the pots themselves. Did Jane Austen utter about teapots as

77. Minton's lively rococo, pattern 3667, Dresden embossed shape c.1840.

she occasionally did about furniture? *See* pp. 61, 62 for books on the various factories' characteristics.

**The Rococo Revival.** Occurring in the 1830s and 40s, this is also a period from which a distinguished collection can still be made. If the ovals were perhaps a bit too severe and controlled for your taste and you prefer something more light-hearted and curvaceous, the neorococo could suit you well. *See* p. 28. These 1830s and 40s pots sometimes stand on outcurving feet but more often on encircling, curvaceously moulded skirts. Handles scroll about, top openings are surrounded by ceramic frills and the whole pot is alive with line and motion, and often the decoration adds more curves and flourishes. Their liveliness is apparent in fig. 77. Many firms made them, in particular, Rockingham, Minton, Spode, Chamberlain's of Worcester, Davenport, Coalport, Ridgway and Grainger's of Worcester. You may well find most examples from the two last-mentioned factories. Many will be marked with pattern numbers. Ridgway pattern numbers for the 1830s and 40s will probably be prefixed numbers ranging from about 2/3211–2/7892, whereas Grainger-Lee reached only 2019 by 1839 and after taking over in 1839 George Grainger started from 1 with the addition of a cross. For Spode

78. Neo-neo rococo late 19th century(?) pattern 7327.

$$\frac{\text{the pattern number}}{150} + 1800$$

gives the approximate date of the introduction of the pattern. Remember that the pattern number normally refers to the decoration and not the shape.

It would be interesting to see a large collection together so that the various sub-groups could be distinguished. You will probably find some extreme examples in neo-neo-rococo like fig. 78 made around 1900 when nearly all the shapes were on offer. Whereas the ovals look well in lines, it could be that these curvaceous pots will look best arranged on shelves above each other as if ready to climb and leap.

**The 1920s and 30s** will prove a far less expensive collecting field so you can afford to be sternly selective and collect only fine examples. It is rather like collecting modern first editions in the sense that the more recent

79. (*top*) Minton's cube, hand-enamelled for Cunard *c*.1930. (*centre*) Octagonal with art deco pattern. (*below*) Royal Doulton with Robin Hood scenes *c*.1937.

80. Doulton printed from drawing by Cecil Aldin, 1927.

81. Maling pottery 'Vine' made for Ringtons Tea Ltd c.1938.

the book is, the more the collector will demand by way of mint condition and untorn dust jacket. But you will set your own rules: that is part of the fun. How far and when do you break them is another matter. Perhaps the most difficult but frequent problem is whether to buy a pot which definitely fills a gap in your collection even if you do not like it.

A collection of this period could show the rather lifeless repro shapes and feeble patterns of much industrial production, the new cubist shapes, the revival of the hand-thrown pot by craftsmen potters and some of the better factory products. You will have to set your own guidelines as to whether to include a pot of each year, make a representative selection or,

82. Transfer prints on Worcester soft paste 1760s.

rather, to collect only what was new in the 20s and 30s. *See* figs. 79(a)–(c).

The catalogues of the Victoria and Albert Museum exhibition of Poole Pottery and of that of Shelley at the Geffrye Museum will be helpful. This collection will need to be made through jumble sales and grotty markets as well as shops and galleries. If such a chase has little appeal and you prefer to be able to collect in a more orderly and certain fashion and buy at planned intervals, you will probably be happier making a collection of late 20th-century teapots. There the challenge will be to choose the best design, the best potting, the truly advanced rather than the merely bizarre.

**Great National Exhibitions.** A very difficult but not impossible collection to attempt would be of teapots shown at the large number of these exhibitions in the 19th century. This should be gripping for a Victorian enthusiast with a taste for the elaborate. There were exhibitions in London in 1851, 1862, 1871, 1872, 1873, 1884, 1885 and 1886; in Manchester in 1887 and in Paris in 1867, 1878 and 1900 and in Glasgow in 1901. Some of the teapots are illustrated in the *Art Journal* and the catalogues of the exhibitions but, unfortunately, the cataloguers mainly preferred to illustrate vases, figures and other decorative items so there will be a good deal of difficulty in tracing many of them. You can start with two shown in the Victoria and Albert booklet *French Exhibition Pieces 1844–78* by Elizabeth Aslin. You will find nearly contemporary background documentation about the factories which made the exhibits in the first really comprehensive history of British ceramics: Llewellynn Jewitt's two-volume *Ceramic Art of Great Britain*, published in 1874.

**Teapots of Single Firms.** Instructive and absorbing collections can be made on this basis. You will need to choose a long-lived firm to give yourself the widest scope. The obvious choices are: Wedgwood, Worcester and Derby factories since the mid-18th century, Minton, Spode and Coalport since the late 18th century, Davenport 1793–1887, Ridgway from about 1802, Grainger's from about 1812 and Allerton's 1859–1942.

Firms' pattern books will be valuable sources. The Spode Shape Book of 1820, for

83. Black print on yellow ground, Staffordshire *c.*1815.

example, illustrates twelve varieties of teapots: the Globe, Low Round Egyptian, Upright Capt, Round Paris, Beaded Déjeuner, Ball, Flower Embossed Low Round, Etruscan, French, Barrel, Old Oval and Round Sweep Neck 'larger to hold eighteen cups'.

The firm of James Sadler of Burslem, who are the largest teapot makers in the country, have been in business since 1882 so should, in theory, illustrate the popular teapot market over the last 100 years but it will be very

84. Highly glossed bright blue with 'griffin' handle, mid to late 19th century.

85. Nottinghamshire stoneware with incised and grit decoration, 18th century.

difficult to date their pots. Other long-lived firms are Cochrans of Glasgow and Malings of Newcastle-on-Tyne (fig. 81).

**Transfer Printed Wares.** If you are keen on these you may want to specialize in teapots bearing topographical prints or the ones showing people. The latter was the theme of a very enjoyable exhibition by the Northern Ceramic Circle *People and Pots* whose catalogue of that title you will certainly need to appreciate how wide this field is. *See* the nostalgic scenes in fig. 82. Most transfer ware is blue on white and there has been a good deal of black on white but lighter blues and greens and browns and purples were favoured in the 1830s and 40s. Fig. 83 shows a fine pot printed in black on a yellow ground.

**Teapots of a Region.** This area of collecting

87. Very rare Derby 'Lady Craveing's Teapot' *c*.1780, a skit on Lady Craven's affairs.

88. Minton's robin designed by Wm Goode for Prince of Wales c.1876.

would provide a pioneering challenge because there is so little documentation about regional pottery and because so much of it is unmarked and difficult to identify. Torquay, Tyneside and Yorkshire potteries have recently been studied (*see* pp. 61, 62 for the histories) and potters have also flourished in Sussex, notably Rye, Devon, around Swansea and in South Derbyshire where many of the large barge teapots with little teapot knobs were made. It is often surprisingly difficult to attribute even characterful country pots like fig. 84 in bright blue. The brown stoneware and salt-glaze traditions still flourishing at Pearson's of Chesterfield and T. G. Green's of Church Gresley serve as a reminder that these traditional wares should be more fully investigated in Derbyshire and Nottinghamshire.

If you are attracted to local studies in your area, consult the museums and local history or

89. Minton's flat iron with cat on handle.

archaeological societies to find out if any work is in progress. Llewellynn Jewitt's *Ceramic Art of Great Britain* (up to 1874) may provide clues. Early trade directories in reference libraries list names of potters. The earliest directory to cover most of the country was the rare *British Universal* published in five volumes in the 1790s.

**Salt-glaze.** If, instead of a region, you were to specialize in a 'body', you could cover a long period in salt-glaze from the mid-18th century houses and camels, through the fine Nottingham wares as in fig. 85 to the Doulton revival of throwing skills in the 1870s and the continuing craftsman tradition since the 1920s.

**Bizarre** teapots are so idiosyncratic, that a collection cannot be expected to show a line of development. We can cherish them as clever

90. Clive Hall's plane.

91. O. Asenbryl's hand-held handle pot, 1975.

92. 'Small Bun' by Crazy Crocks, Halesworth.

or amusing or dismiss them as kitsch. But is it as simple as that? Do they perhaps show the potter's need to be nonconformist or are they a form of protest or, as really seems more likely, are they simply the outcome of one or two jokey designers sparking off others? Certainly the bizarre is in an old tradition ranging from 17th-century Chinese mock branches and 18th-century salt-glaze squirrels via 'Lady Craveing' (fig. 87) and 1870s examples like the robin (fig. 88) and flat iron (fig. 89) to Clarice Cliff's corn cobs and the OKT42 racing cars in the 1930s. There is a current outbreak, including Clive Hall's T46 aeroplane (fig. 90), a gold lustre squirrel by A. Bennett, Carol McNicholl's multi-spouted pots, Woods' long produced elephants and cats, O. Asenbryl's surrealist hand-held handle ((fig. 91) and a witty 'Small Bun' with a cherry knob on the 'icing' lid by Crazy Crocks of Halesworth (fig. 92).

There is, of course, a partial solution to the shortage of collectable teapots. If each of us were to give to our local charity shop or to sell one which we could happily live without, then one man's junk might become another man's treasure and the whole range of collecting would be extended. Similarly, if we each decided to add to our collection the best recently made teapot that we can find or afford, then potters and the ceramic industry – the whole 'incomparable art' – would receive a welcome boost.

# 3. Starting the Collection

93. Lead-glazed
earthenware 'melon' *c.*1760.

TRY to visit one of the large collections listed on page 63 before you begin to buy so that you will develop a standard of quality and see something of the range of possibilities. Look and look and read the literature and look again.

Have you ever stopped to consider how many variable points there are about a teapot? It is necessary to pay attention to the minor details if you are to become a reliable ceramic sleuth. The only satisfactory way to learn is by observing and handling. The handling is not so readily available. You may be able to attend further education classes locally or, if you live in a favoured area like Lambeth or Manchester, join a ceramic circle of enthusiasts (*see* p. 62). Otherwise your best opportunities are at auction salerooms on view days. There you can handle a vast variety of items but do be specially careful: remember you are handling someone else's property. Never pick up items by their handles which may well be defective and do always hold them over the table.

94. New Hall bone china set with prow rim *c.*1810.

95. Creamware, Leeds or Melbourne or Derby 1780s, ribbed baluster shape, striped green.

The small, so-called antiques but rather collectors' fairs which are now a regularly enjoyable feature of Saturday and Sunday life in many parts of the country do bring together the wares of many country and part time dealers. When you visit the larger, more established antiques fairs you will find many dealers, often erudite collectors themselves, ready to discuss their ceramics and enlighten you. It is sound practice to obtain detailed receipts if you buy attributed pieces.

You will find yourself acquiring postcards of teapots and illustrations from auction catalogues and magazine articles. A satisfactory and creative way to store them is in hard backed scrapbooks. Wait until you have a stock so that you can arrange the different subjects and sizes into pleasing and relevant page displays, whether it is like with like or pointing contrasts.

96. Creamware, probably Leeds pottery, early 1770s.

Painstaking collectors fill in index cards about each acquisition with sketch or photograph, dimensions, plan, marks, features, details of where and when bought and price, possible attribution and any relevant details such as 'similar to No. X in the Y

97. Blackware marked Leeds pottery, oval with shaped shoulders and cannon spout 1800–20.

Collection' or 'like Plate A in B's book'. It is worth, at the very least, sticking small labels to the bases of your teapots to record whatever minimal information you have about likely date and maker.

Very many teapots were sold with matching stands but most have become separated from them. Obviously there is added value if the stand is present but as the essential interest is in the pot, it would be self-defeating to buy only those pots which still have their stands.

**Prices.** It is impossible to give accurate, specific guidance as to how much you should expect to pay for an individual item because prices vary according to what the dealer paid for it, what his mark-up needs to be, whether it is his speciality or something he cannot identify, whether he needs to make a quick sale, whether the item is so damaged as to be worth very little or so rare that a little damage is almost irrelevant, whether it is in a currently fashionable collecting field and a host of other factors, none of which need accurately reflect what the teapot would fetch if the collector suddenly needed to sell it.

**Identification.** Fortunately it is possible to find specific information to help you identify the teapots.

## A. MARKED
If they are marked the marks will be mainly of five kinds and a comprehensive book of marks will be helpful.

1. *Name* or *Initials* or *Symbols* – where initials are arranged as in

H & K
T

the lower one usually represents the place of manufacture, as here: Hollinshead & Kirkham, Tunstall.

2. *The Victorian Registration Mark* based on either:

(a) The diamond, in which from 1842–1867 the letter at the top refers to the year and from 1868–1883 the letter on the right. So if there is a letter in the top segment the design was registered before 1868 (fig. 98).

98. Diamond registration marks.

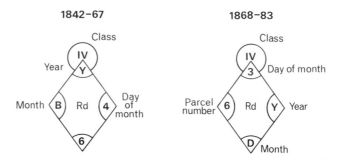

99. Lowestoft ware, Elizabeth Johnson pattern, *c.*1765.

(b) Since 1884 the simple form: Rd No. 123 ... has been used. By 1890 about number 140,000 had been reached; by 1900, 350,000 and by 1910, 550,000. After that fewer designs were registered, the 700,000s being reached only in the 1930s. It is necessary to remember that these marks establish only the date when the pattern was registered; the item may have been made somewhat later.

3. *Words:* The words Limited or Ltd indicate a date after 1861; Trade Mark, 1862 onwards; England, 1891 onwards and still in use; Made in England, after 1900 and probably after about 1910; Bone China, after 1900.

4. *Pattern Numbers and Letters* in several forms:

(a) Simple numbers: 1, 2, 3 ... Most firms started with them and some, including Spode, Davenport and Chamberlain's of Worcester

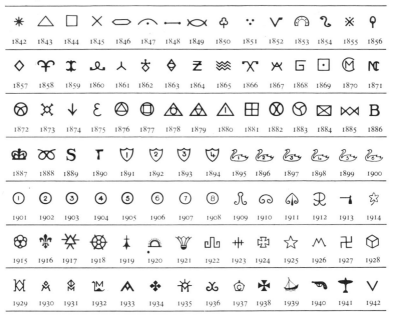

*Impressed marks in use 1842–1942.* *From 1943–68 the last two figures of the year were impressed.*

| 1842 | 1843 | 1844 | 1845 | 1846 | 1847 | 1848 | 1849 | 1850 | 1851 | 1852 | 1853 | 1854 | 1855 | 1856 |
|------|------|------|------|------|------|------|------|------|------|------|------|------|------|------|
| 1857 | 1858 | 1859 | 1860 | 1861 | 1862 | 1863 | 1864 | 1865 | 1866 | 1867 | 1868 | 1869 | 1870 | 1871 |
| 1872 | 1873 | 1874 | 1875 | 1876 | 1877 | 1878 | 1879 | 1880 | 1881 | 1882 | 1883 | 1884 | 1885 | 1886 |
| 1887 | 1888 | 1889 | 1890 | 1891 | 1892 | 1893 | 1894 | 1895 | 1896 | 1897 | 1898 | 1899 | 1900 | |
| 1901 | 1902 | 1903 | 1904 | 1905 | 1906 | 1907 | 1908 | 1909 | 1910 | 1911 | 1912 | 1913 | 1914 | |
| 1915 | 1916 | 1917 | 1918 | 1919 | 1920 | 1921 | 1922 | 1923 | 1924 | 1925 | 1926 | 1927 | 1928 | |
| 1929 | 1930 | 1931 | 1932 | 1933 | 1934 | 1935 | 1936 | 1937 | 1938 | 1939 | 1940 | 1941 | 1942 | |

100. Minton Year Cyphers: marks in use 1880–1975.

seem to have used only these.

(b) Numbers prefixed by a letter: Copeland used D; Minton (became Mintons in 1873) used A or B or G on porcelain and C or E on earthenwares; Royal Worcester B or W and G. Grainger a small x and later G.

(c) Fractional numbers used by Browne-Westhead, Moore and Co., by Coalport up to 2/999 after about 1825 then 3/12 ... and so on up to 8/1,2 ... G. Grainger also used 2/12 ... after the mid-1840s, while Rockingham used only up to about 2/100 or possibly 2/200. John Ridgway used up to 2/9999.

5. *The Cypher or Year Letter* chosen by indi-

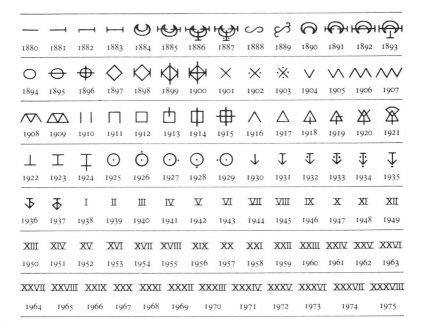

101. Derby Year Cyphers: marks in use 1880–1975.

vidual factories. Those of Minton and Derby are shown above, figs. 100 and 101.

From 1860 Wedgwood impressed three-letter year marks in which the third letter represents the year. They began with O in 1860, carried on to Z and re-started the alphabet in 1872 and 1898. After 1930 the last two numbers of the year, e.g. 34 for 1934, are impressed or painted.

## B. UNMARKED

If the items are unmarked, there are at least twenty points which may need to be considered before a teapot can be attributed. Look

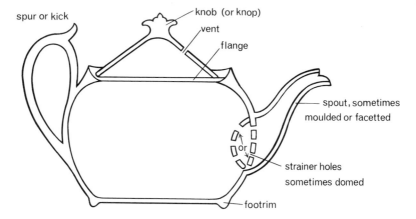

spur or kick

knob (or knop)

vent

flange

spout, sometimes
moulded or facetted

strainer holes
sometimes domed

footrim

102. Sectional diagram of a teapot with lid sitting inside rim.

at the diagram (fig. 102) and note the following points:
1. The body material
2. The overall shape as a guide to period
3. Side profile for position of handle and spout
4. Shape of handle
5. Position on handle of spurs, if any
6. Kind of spout and its decoration
7. Whether the spout is re-inforced anywhere
8. Angle of end of fluting or other moulding on spout
9. Whether opening flanged or not
10. Whether lid fits over body or inside on to flanges
11. Profile of lid
12. Type of knob (or knop)
13. Ground plan of knob
14. Whether or not there is a domed strainer inside
15. How many holes in strainer
16. Plan of base
17. Kind of footrim

18. Height of teapot
19. What painted or printed decoration
20. What moulded decoration

Remember all factories copied and rarely can a single feature clinch an attribution. Here are a few of the kinds of points which, in conjunction with other features, may help you to identify makers:

SPOUTS
The canoe shape whose spout is an integral part of the body – as if drawn out from it – is Coalport.
Early New Hall straight spouts have oak-leaf mouldings on underside.
Long leaf design down top of spout on London shape, Coalport.

HANDLES
Overlapping thumb rests often with scroll mouldings at top of handle, New Hall about 1781–87.

103. A Staffordshire cottage pot, probably *c.*1840.

104. Hornsea pottery,
'Heirloom', 1967.

Early Spode had curved handle with kick at bottom; early Minton had plain loop with flattened top and no kick.

A curved thumb rest at the crest of a handle characteristic of many Miles Mason pots.

Handle shaped like horse's tail joined to a lower leg on Empire style Rockingham.

KNOBS

Steam holes bored through knobs of 'commode' shape, New Hall.

Coronet knobs characteristic of Rockingham neo rococo.

Pineapple or pine cone knobs on New Hall faceted round pots.

Butterfly knops on Ridgway have 5 and 3 spots; on Spode 6 and 4.

Stud-like knobs Worcester about 1780.

Tall 'pagoda' knobs Miles Mason.

BASES

Triangular shaped footrims Lowestoft.

Octagonal teapot stands with flat glazed base Lowestoft.

Early Spode bases flat; early Minton usually recessed with footrim.

Four tiny rosette feet with six petals on some early New Hall.

MISCELLANEOUS

Inside flange of cover glazed on Lowestoft whereas flange of Worcester and Caughley wiped or left free of glaze.

A concave band round some London shapes: R. and Ch. Bourne.

# Books for Further Reading

### Teapots and General

Bedford, J. *Talking about Teapots.*
Draper, J. *18th Century Earthenware Tea and Coffee Pots in the Northamptonshire Museum.*
Greg Collection Catalogue: *The Incomparable Art* (Manchester).
Miller, P. *Teapots and Coffee Pots.*
Sandon, H. *Coffee Pots and Teapots for the Collector.*
Tilley, F. *Teapots and Tea* (mainly re Shand Kydd Coll.).
Victoria and Albert Museum. *Teapots in Pottery and Porcelain.*

---

Bemrose, G. *Nineteenth-Century English Pottery and Porcelain.*
Godden, G. *Illustrated Encyclopaedia of British Pottery and Porcelain. Encyclopaedia of British Pottery and Porcelain Marks. British Pottery and Porcelain 1780–1850. Godden's Guide to English Porcelain.*
Hillier, B. *Pottery and Porcelain 1790–1914* (a social history).
Hughes, G. B. *Country Life Collectors' Pocket-Book of China.*
Lewis, G. *A Collectors' History of English Pottery.*
Wakefield, H. *Victorian Pottery.*

### Types of Body

Blacker, J. F. *The A.B.C. of English Salt-Glaze Stoneware from Dwight to Doulton (1922).*
Garner, F. H./Archer, M. *English Delftwares.*
Grant, M. *The Makers of Black Basaltes.*
Mountford, A. R. *Salt-glazed Stonewares.*
Towner, D. *Creamware.*
Walton, P. *Creamware and other English Pottery at Temple Newsam House.*
Watney, P. *English Blue and White Porcelain of the Eighteenth Century.*

### 1920s and 30s Onwards

Bunt, C. G. *British Potters and Pottery Today* (1956).
Forsyth, G. *20th Century Ceramics* (1937).
Magazines: *The Studio, House and Garden, Ideal Home, Pottery Gazette. Studio Yearbooks.*

### Factories

Berthoud, *M. H. and R. Daniel.*
Cottle, S. (ed) *Maling: a Tyneside Pottery* (Laing Art Gallery, Newcastle).
Degenhardt, R. K. *Belleek.*
Dennis, R. *Doulton Stoneware Pottery 1870–1925.*
Eyles, D. *Doulton Lambeth Wares.*
Godden, G. *Caughley and Worcester Porcelains 1775–1800. Coalport and Coalbrookdale Porcelains. Lowestoft Porcelain. Minton 1793–1850. Ridgway Porcelains.*
Hagger, R. and Adams, E. *Masons Porcelain and Ironstone.*

Hawkins, J. *The Poole Potteries*.
Holgate, D. *New Hall and Its Imitators*.
John, W. D. *Nantgarw Illustrated Porcelain Album. Swansea Porcelain*.
Lockett, T. *Davenport Pottery and Porcelain 1794–1887*.
Mankowitz, W. *Wedgwood*.
Reilly, R. and Savage, G. *A Dictionary of Wedgwood*.
Rice, D. G. *Rockingham Pottery and Porcelain*.
Smith, A. *Liverpool Porcelains*.
Twitchett, J. *Derby Porcelain*.
Watkins, C., Harvey, W., and Senft, R. *Shelley Potteries*.
Whiter, L. *Spode . . . 1733–1833*.

## Transfer Printed Wares

Coysh, A. W. *Blue and White Transfer Ware 1780–1840. Blue Printed Earthenware 1800–1850*.
Williams-Wood, C. *English Transfer Printed Pottery and Porcelain*.

## Regional

Baines, J. M. *Sussex Pottery*.
Bell, R. *Tyneside Pottery*.
Bradley, H. G. *The Ceramics of Derbyshire*.
Fleming, J. A. *Scottish Pottery*.
Lawrence, H. *Yorkshire Potters, Pots and Potteries*.
Lloyd Thomas, D. and E. *Old Torquay Potteries*.
McVeigh, P. *Scottish East Coast Potteries 1750–1840*.

---

# Ceramic Circles and Clubs

Morley College Ceramic Circle, 61 Westminster Bridge Road, London, SE1.
The Northern Ceramic Circle, Hon. Membership Secretary, Bramdean, Jacksons Lane, Hazel Grove, Stockport.
The Royal Doulton International Collectors' Club, 3 Egmont House, 115 Shaftesbury Avenue, London, W1V 7DJ.

# Where Teapots Can Be Seen

Most large museums exhibit some teapots, but specially notable examples and collections are to be seen at:

Victoria and Albert Museum, London SW7.

Pump Room Museum, Harrogate: Holland Child Collection.

Temple Newsam House, Leeds.

Manchester City Art Gallery: Greg Collection.

Milton Manor, Milton, Oxon.

Northampton Museum and Art Gallery.

Castle Museum, Norwich.

City Art Gallery and Museum, Stoke-on-Trent.

*Solutions to quiz on p. 23*

(a) Worcester soft paste, blue scale ground, reserve panels exotic birds *c.*1770.

(b) Wedgwood jasper *c.*1780.   (c) Agate ware, mid-18th century.

(d) Staffordshire salt-glazed stoneware painted in enamels, mid-18th century.

(e) Whieldon/Wedgwood type 'cauliflower' *c.* 1760.   (f) Leeds creamware *c.*1770s.

---

# Acknowledgements

The author and publishers would like to thank the following for permission to use the photographs in this book. Messrs. Christie's 5, 6, 12, 22, 24a&b, 25, 26, 28, 38, 41, 48, 49a, 82, 83, 86, 87; Greg Collection, Manchester City Art Gallery 10, 11, 14, 15, 16, 17, 18, 19, 20; Laing Art Gallery 81; Minton Museum 40, 52, 61, 77, 79, 88, 89; Castle Museum, Nottingham 85; Phillips Auctioneers 21, 23, 27, 37a–e, 51; Royal Doulton International Collectors' Club 56, 57, 58, 60; Messrs. Sotheby's 53, 64; Temple Newsam House 29, 30, 31, 34, 35, 75; Victoria and Albert Museum *Crown Copyright* 1; Wedgwood Museum 32, 33a&b, 50, 54, 59, 65, 68.

For generous help in a variety of ways we are grateful to: Peter Agius, J. Susan Bourne, William Broomhead, A. and A. M. Caiger-Smith, Elizabeth Capper, Craftsman Potters' Association, the Craft Council and Bridget Kinally of the Design Council, Anton Gabszewicz, Derek Halfpenny, Francis Hart, Martin Hunt, Clare Jameson, Joan Jones, Dan Klein, Louise Irvine, David Leach, R. E. K. Leigh, Evelyn Mukherjee, Lynn Miller, J. R. Plant, Rosenthal Studio House, E. J. Sadler, John Sandon, Phyl Wager, William Wake, Peter Walton, E. White and Hilary Wojciechowska.

# Index

**Bold** numbers refer to illustrations